D1542711

USC
TROJANS

BY BARRY WILNER

Published by ABDO Publishing Company, PO Box 398166, Minneapolis, MN 55439. Copyright © 2013 by Abdo Consulting Group, Inc. International copyrights reserved in all countries. No part of this book may be reproduced in any form without written permission from the publisher. SportsZone™ is a trademark and logo of ABDO Publishing Company.

Printed in the United States of America,
North Mankato, Minnesota
052012
092012

Editor: Chrös McDougall
Series Designer: Craig Hinton

Photo Credits: Mark J. Terrill/AP Images, cover, 7, 41; AP Images, 1, 12, 15, 21, 23, 25, 26, 29, 33, 42 (top left), 42 (top right), 42 (bottom); University of Southern California/Collegiate Images via Getty Images, 4, 43 (bottom left); Tom Hauck/AP Images, 8; Mark Lennihan/AP Images, 11; Bettman/Corbis/AP Images, 17; Wally Fong/AP Images, 18, 43 (top); George Long/WireImage/Getty Images, 31; Nick Ut/AP Images, 34; J. Pat Carter/AP Images, 37; Kevork Djansezian/AP Images, 39, 43 (bottom right); Cal Sport Media/AP Images, 44

Library of Congress Cataloging-in-Publication Data
Wilner, Barry.
  USC Trojans / by Barry Wilner.
     p. cm. -- (Inside college football)
  Includes index.
  ISBN 978-1-61783-505-6
  1. University of Southern California--Football--History--Juvenile literature. 2. Southern California Trojans (Football team)--History--Juvenile literature. I. Title. II. Title: University of Southern California Trojans.
  GV958.U5857W55 2013
  796.332'630979494--dc23

                    2012001858

TABLE OF CONTENTS

In 1981, USC tailback Marcus Allen became the fourth Trojan to win the Heisman Trophy.

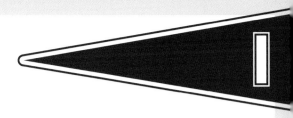

RETURN TO GLORY

THE HEISMAN TROPHY HAS FOUND A HOME AT THE UNIVERSITY OF SOUTHERN CALIFORNIA (USC). THE TROPHY IS GIVEN OUT TO THE BEST COLLEGE FOOTBALL PLAYER EACH SEASON. THROUGH 2011, SEVEN USC TROJANS HAD WON THE TROPHY. NO SCHOOL HAS HAD MORE WINNERS.

The first four USC players to win the Heisman were tailbacks: Mike Garrett in 1965, O. J. Simpson in 1968, Charles White in 1979, and Marcus Allen in 1981. After Allen, no player from USC—or from the West Coast—won the award until 2002. And USC, which had won five national titles during the 1960s and 1970s, also had not won another title during that time.

Quarterback Carson Palmer stopped that trend, though, and changed the momentum. Palmer was one of the nation's most highly recruited high school players in 1997. He was a tall, strong-armed, and smart quarterback. Growing up

INJURED PALMER

When Carson Palmer broke his right collarbone against Oregon early in the 1999 season, he wanted to come back and lead the Trojans later in the year. But coach Paul Hackett had other ideas. Instead, Hackett wanted to let Palmer take the rest of the season to heal. That also would allow Palmer to play an extra year for USC.

"Carson feels good, but he has not been allowed to work his upper body," Hackett said. "Once he can, we'll get a better gauge of how he can throw. I'm looking at it from a medical standpoint. The biggest mistake we can make is to bring him back too soon and damage his arm. I'm not going to take a chance."

It wound up being a wise decision. Palmer got bigger and stronger for his return in 2000. Soon he was one of college football's best players.

in Laguna Niguel, California, Palmer knew all about the great history of USC football. And the USC football coaches knew all about him.

Going to USC has always been special for California kids. Palmer was no different, even though he also thought about Colorado and Notre Dame. But ultimately, his choice was USC.

"It's an excellent school with a great tradition, and it's close to home," Palmer later said about becoming a Trojan. "I thought we could do some great things."

Great things appeared to be ahead for Palmer when he became the starting quarterback for five games as a freshman. The Trojans went 8–5 that season. That earned them a berth in the mid-level Sun Bowl. However, Texas Christian University (TCU) beat the Trojans in that game.

Palmer had a good feeling about the next season. The Trojans got off to a good start, winning their first two

games. They then lost a triple-overtime thriller to Oregon. To make matters worse, Palmer took a hard hit in the game. It broke his right collarbone. The injury ended his season. College athletes are only allowed to play for a maximum of four seasons. However, Palmer was granted a fifth year because his injury came so early in the 1999 season.

Coming back from the injury was difficult for Palmer. He struggled as the full-time starter in 2000. Although he threw for nearly 3,000 yards and 16 touchdowns, he also set a school record with 18 interceptions. The Trojans went 6–6, and coach Paul Hackett was fired.

Palmer had played well, but USC was still stuck in mediocrity. Then Pete Carroll took over as coach in 2001. He had coached the New York Jets and the New England Patriots in the National Football League (NFL).

Pete Carroll took over as USC's coach before the 2001 season and changed the culture within the program.

One of the reasons he decided to come back to college was the opportunity to make the Trojans great again.

Another reason Carroll came aboard was getting to work with Palmer, a talented young quarterback. Carroll changed the offense to make it less complicated. Palmer took to it right away. He had his best season yet, and he cut down his interceptions.

As USC headed into 2002, the always-spirited Carroll was predicting big things, including a Heisman Trophy for Palmer. "He's talented enough to do that, talented enough to be a high first-round draft pick," Carroll said. "I'm thrilled about it and I'll talk to anyone about it."

Palmer and his teammates did their talking on the field—very loudly. USC beat Auburn and eighteenth-ranked Colorado to move up to eleventh in the nation. Palmer totaled two touchdown passes and two touchdown rushes in those games. He became the Trojans' career passing leader the next week against twenty-fifth-ranked Kansas State.

Palmer also threw an interception near the end of the 27–20 loss to Kansas State. But after that game, junior wide receiver Keary Colbert interrupted Palmer's news conference to say he was to blame for that key interception, not Palmer. Many players, Palmer included, said the Trojans became a stronger team after that loss.

USC's schedule did not get any easier. A shutout win over twenty-third-ranked Oregon State was followed by a 30–27 loss to seventeenth-ranked Washington State. In that game, Palmer really caught the nation's attention by completing 32 of 50 passes (career highs) for 381 yards and two touchdowns. He also rushed for a score.

With a 3–2 record, USC was out of the running for the national championship. But the Trojans could still make their mark on the season. They still could win the Pacific-10 Conference title. They were also still in the running to play in a major bowl game, such as the famous Rose Bowl.

Behind Palmer, USC won its next six conference games in a row. Three of those victories were over ranked teams. And only one of

GOING BOWLING

While quarterbacking USC, Carson Palmer took the team to three bowl games. The Trojans lost to TCU 28–19 in the 1998 Sun Bowl in El Paso, Texas. They also lost to Utah 10–6 in the Las Vegas Bowl on Christmas Day in 2001. The biggest bowl game Palmer played in, though, was the Orange Bowl on January 2, 2003. And he shined on the national scene as USC beat Iowa 38–17.

the games, against California, was close. That gave the Trojans a 7–1 conference record. It was good enough for a share of the conference title. Co-Pacific-10 champion Washington State went to the Rose Bowl. And USC was invited to another big game—the Orange Bowl.

Before the bowl games, the Heisman Trophy was given out. Many considered Palmer to be the best player in the country. After all, his 3,820 yards of total offense was a school record. He had six 300-yard passing games. He threw for 33 touchdowns. Plus, he cut his interceptions down from 18 in 2000 to 10. Palmer was the clear leader of Carroll's team. And in the final voting, Palmer easily beat Iowa quarterback Brad Banks for the award.

Soon after, Palmer and his USC teammates arrived in South Florida for the Orange Bowl. The fifth-ranked Trojans were pitted against the third-ranked Iowa Hawkeyes. Palmer finished off an 11–2 season by throwing for 303 yards in the Orange Bowl. USC routed Iowa 38–17.

"I knew we would have a great year," Palmer said. "I don't know if I expected the Orange Bowl, but I knew we would blow it up this

USC quarterback Carson Palmer accepts the Heisman Trophy after his standout season in 2002.

year. We started off slow, and at one point we realized we couldn't lose another game. We kept rolling and rolling and finished off with a bang."

With one incredible season, Palmer had successfully ended USC's 21-year Heisman Trophy drought. And with USC's Orange Bowl win, the Trojans were back on track to soon end the school's national title drought.

Howard Jones became USC's coach in 1925. The team went on to win five Rose Bowls in his 16 seasons.

2

TROJAN TRADITION

COLLEGE FOOTBALL WAS GENERALLY CENTERED IN THE EAST DURING ITS EARLY YEARS. THE USC FOOTBALL TEAM PLAYED ITS FIRST GAME IN 1888. HOWEVER, THE TROJANS FACED ONLY WEST COAST OPPONENTS AND WERE NOT CONSIDERED ANY SORT OF POWER IN THE SPORT.

That changed during the 1920s under coach Elmer Henderson. He led the Trojans to the 1923 Rose Bowl with a 14–3 victory over Penn State. It was their first major win. The Rose Bowl is the oldest and, some say, most prestigious bowl game. It traditionally hosts the Big Ten and Pacific-12 conference champions.

Howard Jones took over as the Trojans' coach in 1925. He had been coaching at Iowa. Notre Dame coach Knute Rockne recommended that USC hire Jones. Rockne was the most famous and powerful coach at the time, so the Trojans took his advice. They would soon be glad they did.

USC went 11–2 and shut out Iowa during Jones's first season. The program also had its first All-American in guard Brice Taylor. There would be hundreds more through the years. Among them was tackle Jesse Hibbs, the first two-time All-American (1927, 1928). Several future College Football Hall of Famers also suited up for the Trojans under Jones. They included halfback/quarterback Morley Drury, end Red Badgro, guard Johnny Baker, and lineman Harry "Blackjack" Smith.

Jones expected perfection from his team. The Trojans went 121–36–13 under him, and they won all five Rose Bowls he led them to. Even with all of that success, Jones remained a very strict coach who was rarely satisfied with how the Trojans practiced or played.

There was no official national champion during college football's early years. Instead, certain organizations selected their own national champion through polls. Various organizations selected USC as national champion four times under Jones—in 1928, 1931, 1932, and 1939.

Perhaps the most lasting tradition Jones started was the rivalry with the Notre Dame Fighting Irish. It did not matter that one team had to spend several days on a train to get to South Bend, Indiana, or to

THE TROJANS

USC adopted the Trojans nickname in 1912. Before that, the team went by nicknames such as the Methodists or the Wesleyans. The school asked *Los Angeles Times* sports editor Owen Bird to choose another nickname. "I came out with an article prior to a showdown between USC and Stanford in which I called attention to the fighting spirit of USC athletes and named them 'Trojan' all the time, and it stuck," Bird said.

Los Angeles each year. As such, USC-Notre Dame became as big as any series in football. The teams have each had their ups and downs over the years, but they still play every year. The winner takes home a trophy called the Jeweled Shillelagh.

USC had lost four of five to Notre Dame when they met in South Bend in 1931. Rockne had died the previous spring in a plane crash. The Trojans won 16–14 on Baker's 33-yard field goal with one minute remaining. That snapped Notre Dame's 26-game unbeaten streak. After the game, Jones took his team to place a wreath at Rockne's gravestone.

Another great rivalry was born in 1936. That is when Jones convinced the crosstown University of California, Los Angeles (UCLA) Bruins to play the Trojans each year. They had met in 1929 and 1930.

TROJAN TRADITION

LA COLISEUM

The Los Angeles Coliseum opened in 1923 with 76,000 seats. USC football became its first regular tenant. The Trojans beat Pomona College 23–7 in October 1923 in the first football game at the stadium. And USC still played there in 2011.

Several other teams and events have called the Coliseum home at various points over the years. The Coliseum has served as the main stadium for two Olympic Games, in 1932 and 1984. UCLA's football team and the NFL's Los Angeles Rams and Los Angeles Raiders once called the stadium home. Even the Los Angeles Dodgers baseball team played there when it first moved from New York in 1958. In fact, World Series games were played at the Coliseum in 1959. The Coliseum also played host to Super Bowl I and Super Bowl VII.

In 1984, the state of California and the US government declared the Coliseum a historic landmark.

However, the Bruins were more like a club team and the Trojans won 76–0 and 52–0. The 1936 game finished 7–7. USC would not lose to UCLA until 1942.

Through 2011, those universities have met every year since 1936 for the Victory Bell. It is a 295-pound (133.8 kg) bell taken from the top of a Southern Pacific locomotive. The winning school paints the bell in its colors: cardinal red for USC or baby blue for UCLA.

Jones died of a heart attack in 1941. Sam Barry coached the team for one year, and then Jeff Cravath took over. By 1943, the Trojans again were strong, although not dominant. Under Jess Hill in 1952, USC went 10–1. The Trojans were ranked second that season when they fell 9–0 to seventh-ranked Notre Dame. But USC beat eleventh-ranked Wisconsin 7–0 in the Rose Bowl to finish fifth in the nation. Aside from that season, the Trojans were never a threat for a national title until John McKay took over in 1960.

Running back Jon Arnett led USC to the 1955 Rose Bowl and was later inducted into the College Football Hall of Fame.

Still, USC had its share of All-Americans during those years. Among those stars were running backs Frank Gifford and Jon Arnett, end Paul Cleary, and tackle John Ferraro. All were later inducted into the College Football Hall of Fame. Dozens of other players would also make their mark at USC after McKay became coach.

Coach John McKay helped USC become a national power—and Tailback U—after taking over in 1960.

3

TAILBACK U

DON CLARK RETIRED AS USC'S COACH AFTER THE 1959 SEASON. THERE WERE SEVERAL MEN ON HIS STAFF WHO SEEMED PREPARED TO TAKE OVER. JOHN MCKAY, THE BACKFIELD COACH FOR ONE YEAR, WAS NOT THE FRONT-RUNNER. BUT HE GOT THE JOB. AND USC SOON BECAME A NATIONAL POWER.

McKay was strong-willed—some would say stubborn—and not always close with his players. He could be quick with a joke with the media. But he was all business and football with his players for much of his 16 seasons as head coach. It proved to be an effective approach.

McKay soon became the winningest coach in USC history. His career record was 127–40–8. That included a 6–3 record in bowl games. In addition, the Associated Press (AP) Poll named USC the national champion in 1962, 1967, and 1972. Another poll by United Press International (UPI) named USC national champion in 1974.

McKay built strong, hard-hitting defenses. He based the offense on the I-formation in the backfield. That involves a fullback beginning each play directly behind the quarterback, and a tailback starting directly behind the fullback. From that formation, the fullback can lead the way as a blocker for the tailback. Using the I-formation, USC became known as Tailback U.

The Trojans did not run the ball all of the time, though. In addition to quarterback Pat Haden, they had some other good quarterbacks and receivers under McKay. But from running back Willie Brown in 1962, through the mid-1970s with Mike Garrett, O. J. Simpson, Clarence Davis, Anthony Davis, and Ricky Bell, USC was known for running the ball. No team ran the sweep better than the Trojans. In that play, the tailback follows his blockers to the outside, and then cuts downfield. Some called the play "Student Body Left" or "Student Body Right," because it seemed like everyone attending USC was blocking for the ball carrier.

McKay brought USC its first AP national championship in 1962. Brown was the team's star that year. The junior tailback also played

STUDENT BODY

USC coach John McKay developed the "Student Body Left" and "Student Body Right" plays to feature his star tailbacks. Blockers on the line would surge to one side of the field or the other—sometimes pulling from the right side to the left or vice-versa. The tailback would take a pitch from the quarterback and then run behind the blockers before breaking downfield. It often was unstoppable.

Mike Garrett was an All-American running back for USC during the 1960s and later became the school's athletic director.

defensive back, lined up as a receiver, and returned kicks. The Trojans had their share of close games. But they also routed Notre Dame 25–0 in the big rivalry game, and then defeated second-ranked Wisconsin 42–37 in the Rose Bowl. It was USC's first Rose Bowl appearance in eight years. They left with an 11–0 record and the national title.

The Trojans did not compete for another championship for a few years. However, another major award came their way in 1965. That is when the short but powerful Garrett, a senior at the time, won the Heisman Trophy. He rushed for 1,440 yards and scored 16 touchdowns.

TAILBACK U

Garrett also began the USC tradition of running out every play in practice. In the past, running backs would stop when they were touched on a play in practice. Under Garrett, they began running to the end zone on each play.

Perhaps the most famous of all of USC's tailbacks came along next: Simpson. He transferred from City College of San Francisco to USC in 1967. In his first season at USC, Simpson was the spark plug for a second national title. He rushed for 1,415 yards and scored 11 touchdowns. The Trojans went 10–1, losing only to an Oregon State team that was nicknamed "giant killers." The 3–0 loss was played in rain and mud. Some wondered if USC was looking ahead to playing city rival UCLA the next week.

Although USC slipped from the number one ranking with that loss, a win over the newly first-ranked UCLA could lift the Trojans back to the top. Simpson was ready. McKay called his favorite play—23-blast. And Simpson indeed blasted through the left side of the line for a 64-yard touchdown. That lifted USC to a thrilling 21–20 victory and a berth

McKAY'S SONS

John McKay's two sons also have had a long history in football. Rich McKay is the president of the NFL's Atlanta Falcons. He is also co-chairman of the league's competition committee, which helps set rules. J. K. McKay played at USC from 1972 to 1974 as a wide receiver. He also played in the NFL and works at USC in the athletic department.

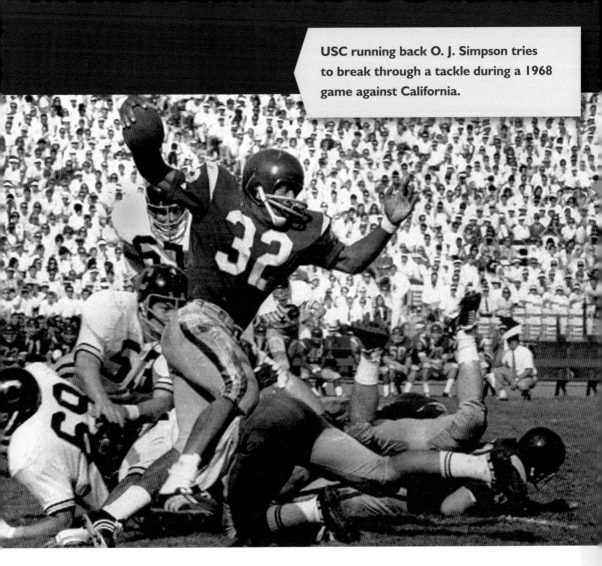

in the Rose Bowl. There, the Trojans beat fourth-ranked Indiana. Once again, USC was named the national champion.

Simpson was not done with his star turn. In 1968, "The Juice," as he had been nicknamed, was the country's most dominant player. He rushed for a then-record 1,709 yards, returned kickoffs, and scored 22 touchdowns. Then he won the Heisman Trophy. The editor of the *Chicago American* newspaper said Simpson was better than Red Grange. Many consider Grange the greatest college football runner ever.

TAILBACK U

NOTRE DAME-USC

On November 30, 1974, Notre Dame surged to a 24–0 lead at USC when, suddenly, the Trojans woke up. USC came back and scored 55 straight points in 17 minutes.

Late in the first half, USC star tailback Anthony Davis caught a seven-yard touchdown pass from quarterback Pat Haden. However, the extra point was blocked and the half ended 24–6. Then Davis really got the Trojans rolling. He took a kickoff two yards deep in the end zone, raced upfield, cut left, and scored his sixth kick return touchdown, making it 24–12. Davis also scored a few minutes later from the 6-yard line. Then, after Notre Dame fumbled, he again scored—and added a two-point conversion. Just 6:23 into the third period, USC led 27–24.

The Trojans were not done, either. USC had three touchdown catches plus an interception returned 58 yards for another to finish off the 55–24 rout.

Simpson moved on to the NFL as the first pick in the next year's draft. Clarence Davis replaced him at USC. In his two seasons as the main tailback, Davis ran for 2,323 yards and scored 21 total touchdowns. Like Simpson, he also ran back kicks. But unlike Simpson, he did not lead USC to a national championship. The Trojans went 16–4–2 in his two seasons, finishing third in 1969.

Anthony Davis came along next. He was successful in getting the Trojans back to the top. Perhaps the most spectacular of USC's backs, Davis also was a brilliant kick returner. In 1972, USC cruised through its schedule for 12 victories. The Trojans outscored their opponents 467–134. The sophomore Davis scored 16 rushing touchdowns. Six of those came in one game against Notre Dame. The 1972 Trojans capped off the season by beating number three Ohio State in the Rose Bowl to claim the national title.

USC running back Anthony Davis rushes for a first down during a 1974 game at the LA Coliseum.

Davis added another 26 rushing touchdowns in his next two seasons. He capped his career in one of the greatest comebacks in USC history. Davis scored four touchdowns and a two-point conversion as USC came back from 24–0 to beat fifth-ranked Notre Dame 55–24.

"It's the best all-round game I've played," Davis said. "I did everything well. I caught passes, ran from scrimmage, returned kickoffs, and even blocked pretty well."

USC finished 10–1–1 and split the national title with Oklahoma in 1974. McKay coached one more season before leaving to coach the NFL's Tampa Bay Buccaneers. But the Trojans would not slow down without him.

TAILBACK U

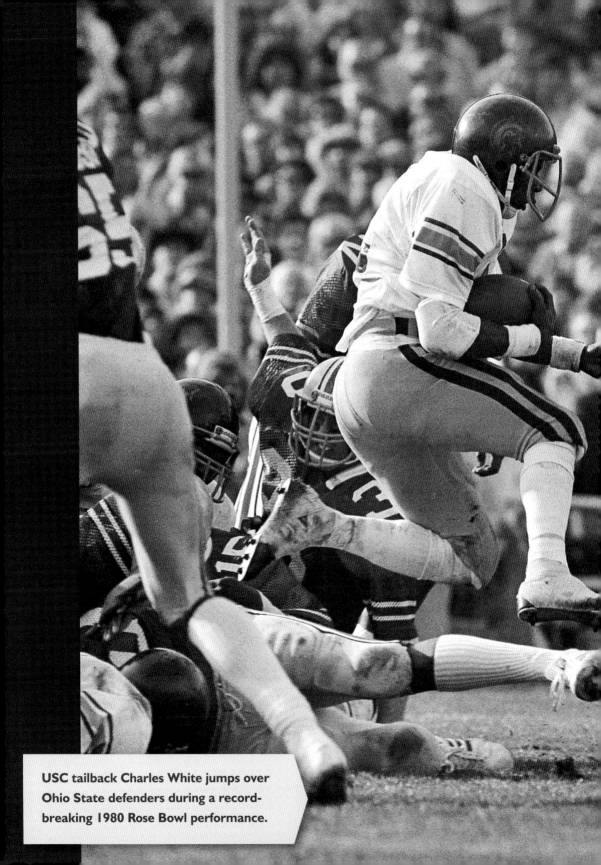

USC tailback Charles White jumps over
Ohio State defenders during a record-
breaking 1980 Rose Bowl performance.

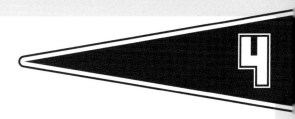

4

STAYING ON TOP

THE WINNING CONTINUED FOR USC. IN FACT, USC'S NEXT HEAD COACH, JOHN ROBINSON, WOULD GO ON TO THE COLLEGE FOOTBALL HALL OF FAME.

Robinson had been USC's offensive coordinator from 1972 to 1974. He left for one season to work in the NFL, and then he was asked to come back and replace McKay. It was a smart choice. Robinson had a career record of 104–35–4 during two periods coaching at USC. His teams went to eight bowl games and won the 1978 UPI national championship.

During that time, the Trojans had 24 All-Americans, 22 NFL first-round draft picks, and two Heisman Trophy winners in tailbacks Charles White and Marcus Allen. USC also went 4–0 in the Rose Bowl.

"Somebody's gonna carry the ball 30 times a game," Robinson said. "I'm gonna put up a stand next to those other Heisman Trophies and get someone to fill it."

Robinson's teams certainly featured great running games, starting with Ricky Bell's 1,417 rushing yards in 1976. But the Trojans also had stars at nearly every position. These included linebacker Clay Matthews and his brother, offensive lineman Bruce Matthews, as well as linebacker Dennis Johnson and defensive back Ronnie Lott.

"You need a balanced offense, but the running game is the foundation," he said.

Still, Robinson's first game as head coach at USC did not go very well. The Trojans lost 46–25 at home to unranked Missouri. No matter, Robinson figured. His team would come around. And it did— immediately. USC routed Oregon 53–0 the next week. The Trojans won every remaining game on the schedule to finish 11–1 and ranked third. A 14–6 victory over second-ranked Michigan in the Rose Bowl helped the Trojans wind up second in the nation.

In one span, from October 1978 to mid-November 1980, the Trojans were unbeaten in 28 games. In 1978, the only blemish was a

1980 ROSE BOWL

USC was ranked third when it faced top-ranked Ohio State on New Year's Day of 1980 in one of the most exciting Rose Bowls. Heisman Trophy winner Charles White, running behind All-American tackle Anthony Munoz much of the time, gained 71 of the 83 yards on the winning drive in the final quarter, scoring from the 1-yard line. Eric Hipp kicked the decisive extra point in USC's 17–16 victory. White gained 247 yards on 39 carries.

USC players carry coach John Robinson off the field after a win in the Rose Bowl following the 1979 season.

20–7 midseason loss at Arizona State. USC rampaged through the rest of its schedule, beating fifth-ranked Michigan 17–10 in the Rose Bowl. USC earned UPI's portion of the national title. But the AP went for Alabama.

USC was 6–1 against Notre Dame and 5–2 against UCLA in its main rivalry games during Robinson's early era. The Trojans were almost

SPLIT NATIONAL TITLE

Before the Bowl Championship Series (BCS) began in 1999, the national champions were decided by polls. Sportswriters and broadcasters voted in the AP Poll. Coaches made the choice in the UPI Poll, and later, in the ESPN Poll.

From 1970 through 2003, split champions happened eight times. USC was involved in three of those. The Trojans won the coaches' poll in 1974 and 1978, while the media voted for Oklahoma in 1974 and Alabama in 1978. It turned around in 2003. USC got the AP nod, and Louisiana State University (LSU) won the coaches' poll (and the BCS).

Alabama and Nebraska have also been involved in split championships more than once since 1970. In 1973, the AP voted for Notre Dame, and the coaches selected Alabama. And in 1978, Alabama and USC split. Nebraska won the AP and Texas won the UPI in 1970. And in 1997, Michigan won the AP and Nebraska won the UPI.

always strong and physical on defense, they passed the ball pretty well, and they had great special teams. But their calling card remained the run.

The three great tailbacks under Robinson were Bell, White, and Allen. Bell was at first a fullback. However, Robinson moved him to tailback when he saw how well Bell broke tackles and how much speed he had. Bell never seemed to tire. In one game as a senior against Washington State, he carried the ball 51 times for 347 yards. He was runner-up for the Heisman Trophy behind Pittsburgh's Tony Dorsett.

White was not as big or as powerful as Bell. But few USC runners got to the outside as well. Once he reached the open field, he was gone. He also was remembered for his dives over the pile and into the end zone. White scored 49 touchdowns in his career, finishing as the Pacific-10's career rushing leader (6,245 yards). USC went 42–6–1 with White in the lineup.

"Charlie was the toughest, most intense running back I've ever coached," said Robinson of the 1979 Heisman Trophy winner. White sparked USC to a thrilling 17–16 victory over top-ranked Ohio State in the Rose Bowl that year. The Trojans finished number two, behind Alabama.

White hardly was the last great USC tailback. Allen had moves as smooth as O. J. Simpson's and big-play skills that were as good as anyone

STAYING ON TOP

USC had seen. Allen started out as a defensive back, but soon it was clear he needed to be carrying the ball and he switched to tailback.

Allen backed up White for two seasons. Then he became a starter as a junior in 1980. Allen rushed for 1,563 yards and scored 14 touchdowns that year. But it was only a taste of what Allen could do. The next year, he broke 14 national records while rushing for 2,342 yards and scoring 23 touchdowns. Allen won pretty much every award for which he was eligible, including the Heisman Trophy.

Robinson left for the NFL's Los Angeles Rams in 1983. USC had been ranked at the end of every season under him. Ted Tollner replaced Robinson as USC coach. Tollner stayed for four seasons, and then Larry Smith was in charge for six. While Robinson was turning his professional team into winners, the Trojans were struggling. They went 70–45–4 in that decade without him. Instead of regular visits to the Rose Bowl, they often were playing in lesser games, such as the John Hancock or Freedom Bowls.

The school wanted a return to glory—so Robinson returned in 1993. But his second stint was not nearly as successful. Off-field problems hurt the program throughout. USC even fell to 6–6 and then 6–5 in his final two years. There was no return to glory and no competing for national titles.

That would have to wait until Pete Carroll arrived, bringing along the likes of Reggie Bush, Mike Williams, Matt Leinart, and Mark Sanchez.

STAYING ON TOP

USC wide receiver Kareem Kelly makes a leaping catch for a touchdown during a 1999 game against UCLA.

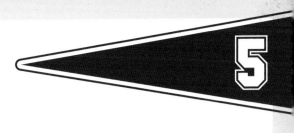

UNBEATABLE USC

FOR DECADES, THE PACIFIC-8 CONFERENCE—WHICH BECAME THE PACIFIC-10 IN 1978 AND PACIFIC-12 IN 2011—NORMALLY BELONGED TO USC. BY THE TURN OF THE CENTURY, THOUGH, EVERY SCHOOL IN THE CONFERENCE HAD IMPROVED ENOUGH THAT THE TROJANS NO LONGER DOMINATED.

Paul Hackett replaced John Robinson as coach in 1997. USC continued getting players who would be high NFL Draft picks. But the Trojans were not finishing very high in the conference or the national rankings. All of that changed after Hackett was fired following a 5–7 season in 2000.

In came Pete Carroll. His experience was mostly in the NFL. Carroll brought with him a lively, confident style. Now he needed to bring USC back up to the top. He already had some key players. Juniors such as quarterback Carson Palmer, wide receiver Kareem Kelly, and running back Sultan McCullough were established stars. Two freshmen defensive

LOFA TATUPU

Mosi Tatupu was one of the toughest, hardest-working Trojans when he played in the mid-1970s. His son, Lofa Tatupu, was not quite the same star as a linebacker and quarterback at King Philip Regional High School in Wrentham, Massachusetts, where Mosi was the coach.

Lofa wound up in college at Maine, which played one division lower than the top rung of college football. Lofa did not want to stay at Maine, but many bigger schools said they were not interested in bringing him in as a transfer. So Mosi sent tapes of Lofa to USC coach Pete Carroll. It was not until a week before the semester began in 2002 that USC invited Lofa to join the team. He then had to sit out a season per college rules. By 2003, though, he led the national champion Trojans in tackles. The next year, he was an All-American and USC won another national title.

linemen, Mike Patterson and Kenechi Udeze, were major players too. But Carroll needed more.

The Trojans went 6–6 in Carroll's first season. Meanwhile, his assistants searched for the kind of talent that would again make USC a champion. They would soon find them. In 2002, Palmer led the Trojans to an 11–2 record. That included a rout of Iowa in the Orange Bowl. Palmer also won USC's first Heisman Trophy since 1981.

That was exciting, but not enough. Carroll and his players wanted more— another national title. They began the 2003 season strong. The number-one ranking was in range. The third-ranked Trojans had won 11 in a row and could almost taste it. But then they tasted defeat—bitter defeat.

USC was down by three at unranked California. Trojans kicker Ryan Killeen kicked a 33-yard field goal with 16 seconds left to send the game to overtime. But in the third overtime,

Lofa Tatupu celebrates after sacking Oklahoma quarterback Jason White during the 2005 BCS title game.

Killeen missed a 39-yarder. Then Cal made a 38-yard field goal to win 37–34.

Not much would get away from USC during the rest of the year—or in future years. USC ran the table, scoring at least 37 points in every game to take the Pacific-10 title. A 52–28 romp past Oregon State got the Trojans the nation's top ranking in the AP Poll. They played fourth-ranked Michigan in the Rose Bowl with a chance for their first national crown since 1978.

It was a chance they would not let slip. USC beat the Wolverines 28–14 to confirm the AP's top ranking. However, the end of the season was mired in controversy. Because college football does not have a playoff, there were split champions, with LSU being the BCS's choice.

USC was loaded with talent, though. The Trojans were favored to win all the trophies in 2004. Although they had some close calls, they were ranked number one all season. All USC had to do was beat the Oklahoma Sooners in the Orange Bowl to again be the undisputed national champions. And beat them they did. Junior Heisman Trophy-winning quarterback Matt Leinart led the way. He threw for 332 yards and had four touchdown passes by halftime. Second-ranked Oklahoma had not allowed a touchdown in its final three regular-season games. The USC defense gave up only 82 yards to Oklahoma's All-American running back Adrian Peterson. USC won 55–19.

Leinart had to decide whether to join the NFL early. He ended up returning to USC for his senior season. That meant the best backfield in the country, including juniors Reggie Bush and LenDale White, would

2003 SPLIT TITLE

Pete Carroll had a simple reaction to splitting the 2003 national championship with BCS winner LSU. "How do you top this? How about doing it again a couple times?" Carroll said after being presented the AP championship trophy. "It's so great to be standing in front of you representing what this university has always been about: winning championships, national championships."

From left, Reggie Bush, Darnell Bing, Matt Leinart, and Dallas Sartz approach the field for the 2005 season opener.

return. Bush and White did not yet meet the NFL's age requirements. That backfield group helped the Trojans again stay atop the rankings for the entire schedule before meeting second-ranked Texas in the Rose Bowl.

During that season, USC scored 51 or more points seven times. Its closest win was an epic game at ninth-ranked Notre Dame in October. Trailing 31–28 in the final seconds, the Trojans fumbled out of bounds as

the clock wrongly expired. After some confusion, the clock was reset
to seven seconds. The ball was placed at Notre Dame's 1-yard line, and
USC had one more chance.

Carroll could have ordered a tying field goal to go to overtime, but
that was not how his teams operated. They wanted to win. Leinart tried
a quarterback sneak and, with Bush pushing from behind, he surged into
the end zone for the victory.

Fans had been waiting for a USC-Texas showdown all year. Both
teams went undefeated through the regular season. Players from those
teams also took the top three places in the Heisman Trophy voting. Bush
won the trophy, while Leinart finished third. Meanwhile, Texas junior
quarterback Vince Young was second. Young showed why he was second
in the national title game. Although the Trojans scored 38 points, the
Longhorns got 41 and the victory.

Carroll's teams went 97–19 until 2010, when he returned to the
NFL. USC had several talented players during that time, including
quarterbacks John David Booty and Mark Sanchez. But the Trojans did

USC DYNASTY

A dynasty in sports comes when one team is on top for a long time. USC football from
2003 to 2005 was that strong. "We're definitely on our way to qualifying as a dynasty,"
All-American sophomore running back Reggie Bush said after the 2004 national title.
Although they did not win the 2005 championship, losing it to Texas in the Rose Bowl, the
Trojans were 37–2 in that three-year span.

USC quarterback Mark Sanchez runs the ball against Arizona during a 2007 game.

not win another national championship under Carroll. And when he left, the Trojans were about to go on probation for violations that also wound up stripping Bush of his 2005 Heisman Trophy.

Lane Kiffin, another former professional coach and ex-assistant to Carroll, replaced him at USC. Kiffin inherited the punishments when he took over, including a two-year ban on playing in any bowl games. But the Trojans' winning tradition continued. They improved from 8–5 in Kiffin's first season to 10–2 in 2011. It was further proof that the USC Trojans remained a national power.

[41]

TIMELINE

USC plays its first two games, which are both shutout victories over the Alliance Athletic Club.

Under Elmer Henderson, the Trojans go 10–1 and win the Rose Bowl 14–3 over Penn State on January 1, 1923.

Howard Jones is hired as coach. He goes on to make USC a football power.

Thanks to Jones's friendship with Knute Rockne, he arranges an annual series between USC and Notre Dame. The Fighting Irish win the first meeting 13–12.

With no official national title, USC is declared champion by several outlets after a 9–0–1 record. USC again wins the title in 1931 and 1932.

1888 **1922** **1925** **1926** **1928**

Tailback Mike Garrett becomes USC's first Heisman Trophy winner.

Led by O. J. Simpson, whose 64-yard run lifts them past top-ranked UCLA. The Trojans later win another national championship.

USC goes 12–0, outscoring opponents 467–134 for the season. A 42–17 rout of Ohio State in the Rose Bowl earns the Trojans another national crown.

USC splits the national championship with Oklahoma after going 10–1–1, edging Ohio State 18–17 in the Rose Bowl.

John Robinson's first USC team goes 11–1 and beats Michigan in the Rose Bowl. The Trojans win a Rose Bowl rematch and another shared national title in 1978.

1965 **1967** **1972** **1974** **1976**

The annual series with UCLA begins, and the teams tie 7–7.

Jones's last national champion team goes 8–0–2, tying Oregon and UCLA. A 14–0 win over Tennessee in the Rose Bowl finishes the season.

Frank Gifford becomes the first star running back at what will become known as Tailback U.

John McKay is hired to replace Don Clark as coach. McKay will become USC's winningest coach (127–40–8).

The Trojans capture the national title, beating Wisconsin 42–37 in one of the most famous Rose Bowl games on January 1.

1936 1939 1951 1960 1963

Marcus Allen sets 14 national records, rushing for 2,342 yards and scoring 23 touchdowns to win the Heisman Trophy.

Carson Palmer wins the Heisman Trophy. He is the first West Coast player honored since Allen.

USC caps a 12–1 season with a 28–14 win over Michigan for another shared national title.

Matt Leinart wins the Heisman Trophy and USC repeats as champions, beating Oklahoma 55–19 in the Orange Bowl.

Carroll leaves USC for the NFL after posting a 97–19 record. Lane Kiffin takes over amid sanctions.

1981 2002 2003 2004 2010

QUICK STATS

PROGRAM INFO

University of Southern California
    Methodists, Wesleyans (1888–1911)
University of Southern California
    Trojans (1912–)

NATIONAL CHAMPIONSHIPS
(* DENOTES SHARED TITLE)

1928*, 1931, 1932, 1939*, 1962, 1967,
1972, 1974*, 1978*, 2003*, 2004

OTHER ACHIEVEMENTS

BCS bowl appearances (1999–): 7
Pacific-12 Conference titles (1922–): 37
Bowl Record: 32–16

KEY PLAYERS
(POSITION[S]; SEASONS WITH TEAM)

Marcus Allen (RB; 1978–81) †
Jon Arnett (RB; 1954–56)
Reggie Bush (RB; 2003–05) †
Anthony Davis (RB; 1972–74)
Mike Garrett (RB; 1963–65) †
Frank Gifford (HB; 1949–51)
Matt Leinart (QB; 2002–05) †
Ronnie Lott (DB; 1977–80)

Carson Palmer (QB; 1998–2002) †
O. J. Simpson (RB; 1967–68) †
Harry "Blackjack" Smith (DL/OL;
    1937–39)
Charles White (RB; 1976–79) †
Ron Yary (T; 1965–67)
    † denotes Heisman Trophy winner

KEY COACHES

Pete Carroll (2001–09):
    97–19; 7–2 (bowl games)
John McKay (1960–75):
    127–40–8; 6–3 (bowl games)
John Robinson (1976–82, 1993–97):
    104–35–4; 7–1 (bowl games)

HOME STADIUM:

Los Angeles Coliseum (1923–)

* All statistics through 2011 season

Popular comic actor and USC grad Will Ferrell might be the Trojans' biggest fan. Ferrell became friendly with Pete Carroll when Carroll was coaching at USC. Ferrell would attend practices and stand on the sideline for games at the Coliseum. During one of those practices just before Halloween in 2008, a man fell from a platform and another man ran across the field on fire. Turns out, it was Ferrell pulling a prank in which he carried the "injured" man to safety.

Frank Gifford became best known as a broadcaster on *Monday Night Football*. But he also was an outstanding college and professional football player. At USC, Gifford played both offense and defense. He was an All-American in 1951, when he led USC in rushing with 841 yards. Gifford also was a placekicker and could throw the ball well. In 1950, he had three interceptions as a defensive back.

"There is no question in my mind that USC is the best team in the country and may be the best team in the history of college football." —Stanford coach Jim Harbaugh before the 2007 season. But USC went just 11–2 that year.

President Warren G. Harding was scheduled to officially open the Los Angeles Coliseum on August 2, 1923. But Harding caught pneumonia on a trip to Alaska in July, and was too ill to attend. In fact, he died 30 minutes before he would have dedicated the stadium where the Trojans have played since it opened.

[45]

GLOSSARY

All-American
A player chosen as one of the best amateurs in the country in a particular sport.

club team
A team that is not officially sanctioned by a school.

conference
In sports, a group of teams that plays each other each season.

draft
A system used by professional sports leagues to select new players in order to spread incoming talent among all teams. The NFL draft is held each spring.

dynasty
A team that wins many championships in a short period of time.

momentum
A continued strong performance based on recent success.

probation
A period of time where a person or team tries to make up for wrongdoing.

recruited
Persuaded a player to come to a certain school to play on its team. A player being sought is known as a recruit.

retire
To officially end one's career.

rivalry
When opposing teams bring out great emotion in each team, its fans, and its players.

undisputed
Not questioned.

upset
A result in which the supposedly worse team defeats the supposedly better team.

FOR MORE INFORMATION

FURTHER READING

Rappoport, Ken. *The Trojans.* Huntsville, AL: Strode Publishing, 1974.

Travers, Steven. *The USC Trojans.* Lanham, MD: Taylor Trade Publishing, 2010.

Wharton, David. *USC Football: Yesterday and Today.* Lincolnwood, IL: Publications International, 2009.

WEB LINKS

To learn more about the USC Trojans, visit ABDO Publishing Company online at **www.abdopublishing.com**. Web sites about the Trojans are features on our Book Links page. These links are routinely monitored and updated to provide the most current information available.

PLACES TO VISIT

College Football Hall of Fame
111 South St. Joseph St.
South Bend, IN 46601
1-800-440-FAME (3263)
www.collegefootball.org

This hall of fame and museum highlights the greatest players and moments in the history of college football. Among the former Trojans enshrined here are Marcus Allen, Mike Garrett, and coach John McKay.

Los Angeles Coliseum
3939 South Figueroa Street
Los Angeles, CA 90037
213-747-7111
www.lacoliseumlive.com

This has been USC's home field since 1923.

USC Trojans Athletic Hall of Fame
University Park Campus
University of Southern California
Los Angeles, CA 90089
213-740-2311
www.usc.edu

This is a hall of fame and museum honoring great athletes from all sports who played at USC.

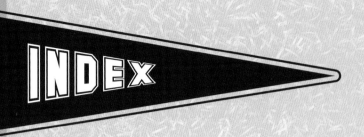

INDEX

ABOUT THE AUTHOR

Barry Wilner has been a sportswriter for the Associated Press since 1976. He has covered every Super Bowl since 1985, nine World Cups, 12 Olympic Games, plus the Stanley Cup finals, championship boxing matches, major golf and tennis tournaments, and auto races. Wilner has written several books and also teaches journalism at Manhattanville College in Purchase, New York. He and his wife have four children and one grandchild.